IMPORTANCE OF THE ROLE OF FATHERHOOD AND ENTREPRENEURSHIP TO STRENGTHEN COMMUNITIES

7 Steps to Strengthen Communities

The interconnectedness between
fathers and entrepreneurship

JASON MURRAY

*Jason
Murray*

12/17/22

Printed in the United States of America

First Printing, 2019

ISBN: 9780578507743

Edited & Formatted by Show Your Success
Published by Jason Murray

About the Author

JASON MURRAY – FINANCIAL SERVICES ENTREPRENEUR/SALES & MARKETING CONSULTANT/AUTHOR

Jason Murray, is a father, grandfather, entrepreneur, community servant, organizational leader and author. Raised in the Bronx, NY by a single parent, Murray achieved scholastic success in school and developed business skills, marketing acumen and consultative aptitude in the corporate world which spanned three decades, working in the consumer goods, publishing, pharmaceutical, healthcare and financial services industries.

The corporate world gave Jason the ability to foster and develop numerous relationships nationally and instilled in him the importance of business expansion and economic development through challenging experiences and consistent career advancement. Now, currently a serial entrepreneur, consultant and thought leader, Murray is charged with providing a blueprint for success by strengthening communities and narrowing the wealth gap through entrepreneurship education, leadership skills development and spiritual growth.

Murray is a graduate of Marist College, with a B.S in Business Administration and a Concentration in Marketing.

Jason became a widower at an early age, thus was a single parent himself for 3 years. He currently resides in Teaneck, NJ with his wife, Tanya. He raised six children through a blended family and has nine grandchildren, which gives him a clear understanding of his ever-evolving legacy!

Dedication

I would like to dedicate this book to a number of individuals who are very special to me and have had an impact on my life as well as inspired me to write this book to share with individuals and aspiring entrepreneurs.

My wife, life partner and friend for over 40 years, Tanya Moore-Murray has been by my side as we have raised our family and nurtured a loving relationship through our blessed union. My wife, Rhonda Fishburne Murray, who preceded me in death, the mother of my first two children, whose spirit and legacy lives today through the life of our children and grandchildren. My children and grandchildren who have provided me with a sense of purpose as a father and grandfather and their loving support exhibited in many ways through the years.

My mother, Elizabeth Murray, who raised me, gave me an example of handling fiscal responsibility and business acumen at an early age through my progression to becoming an adult and showed society how an individual can overcome being a single parent and successfully raising a family. My brother, B. Desmond Murray aka Bakari Adeyemi, who provided me an excellent example of being a community servant, college administrator and what it truly means to be a brother, friend and role model. My parents in love, Elaine and Gilbert Moore, who have always viewed me as their son and showed me their sense of family while always being supportive grandparents.

My spiritual leader, Rev. Dr. Lester W. Taylor, Jr., who has been a guiding force for my spiritual growth and was available for counsel when my wife Tanya and myself were raising our children.

And lastly, my ancestors, father, James Murray, Jr., grandparents, Nettie and Harrison Bradley, grandparents, Sarah and James Murray, Sr., who are looking over us and were responsible for giving my parents life who ultimately gave me life, enabling me to become the individual I am through administering my God given talents.

Acknowlegments

I would also like to acknowledge the following supporters who were instrumental in the creation of this book:

Derek Maillard

Keith Williams

Thomas Tipton

Esmeralda Mena

Jonah Eddy Denizard

Gregory Denizard

Adrian Jones

Stephen Urquhart

Angela Davis

Deyami Murray

Charisma DeZonie

Taurea Vision Avant

Preface

We now live in very challenging times. At the same time, there are many opportunities available for those who stay the course, persevere and reach for success in developing themselves personally and professionally. One of the major problems our society faces today is the rising divorce rate, which increases the rate of single headed households, ultimately creating instability in our communities.

Whether you are raised in a single-parent household or two parent household, you must create for yourself a path for success in life. My upbringing by my mother, Elizabeth Murray afforded me the opportunity to be raised by a banker, thus I was exposed to an understanding of fiscal responsibility at a young and early age. She gave me the discipline, sense of purpose and knowledge of focusing on our necessities as a priority opposed to our wants because we had to make ends meet on a limited income. Having the foundation and presence of God in our lives, gave us the ability to weather many storms.

My reason for writing this book is to provide a formula for success to lead a balanced life, raise a family and encourage entrepreneurship as an option for unlimited income potential. To do so, it will require leadership skills, a high level of self-esteem and mental toughness, which will enable individuals to create a legacy which they can be proud of. My mentors which shared with me while I was a teenager how to be a man, develop mental toughness and strength in character as well as giving back to society, assisted me with solidifying myself as an individual determined to be the best I can be.

The 7 Steps for Strengthening Communities through Entrepreneurship has many lessons and is intended to show an individual that you can make it in life despite any obstacle in your way as long as you stay focused, adhere to a mindset for growth, and allow your God giving talents keep you striving for success. Leaving a legacy is one of the most important aspects of life for individuals. What will be your Legacy?

I was raised in a single parent household in the Bronx, NY during the sixties and seventies when gangs were a major force in our community. Because my brother and I did not have a father figure in the house to lead us and guide our decision-making, we could have easily been persuaded to join one of the many local gangs. Fortunately for us, our mother, who served as a mother and father figure, kept us focused and she kept us involved in community activities to shield us from the effects of peer pressure. After-school programs, and sleep away camps during the summer and vacations, showed us life outside of the inner city and past the South Bronx.

The most profound experience I had as a teenager was being introduced to a rites of passage program focused on leadership development, community awareness, discipline, strength in character and the importance of Brotherly love. My pledging experience in the seventies to the Order of the Feather Fraternity and my involvement with Camp Minis-ink instilled in me the necessary skills to become a leader, take initiatives and most importantly, the foundation to develop into a successful thought leader, and community servant. It prepared me to effectively lead my family and become a successful businessman.

The Senior Deans, who brought our line through our initiation process, guided us to understand our strengths, capabilities and full potential. This rites of passage experience as a teenager enabled me to make the transition from adolescent to manhood and prepared me to handle adversity and challenges in life as a young adult. For me personally, the Senior Deans also served as father figures and gave me role models to look up to at a time when I was searching for my identity and seeking direction from a male perspective. Therefore, I thank Rodney Beckford and Kenneth Bolt for instilling in me the leadership skills which I not only benefit from today, but would like to now share with others who may be seeking direction to successfully lead their families, become a successful businessman and make an impact in our society.

Tabe of Contents

CHAPTER ONE

Family Gives Meaning to Work

"The graveyard is the richest place on earth, because it is here that you will find all the hopes and dreams that were never fulfilled, the books that were never written, the songs that were never sung, the inventions that were never shared, the cures that were never discovered, all because someone was too afraid to take that first step, keep with the problem, or determined to carry out their dream."
—*Les Brown*

You have full control of your destiny

You have full control of your destiny if you are able to make decisions on your own, without money being an issue when you make those decisions and if you know exactly who you want to be. You have full control of your destiny if you have obtainable goals and the knowledge that based on your own efforts and resources, you will be able to reach these goals.

You have full control of your destiny when you have freedom and flexibility of time, and have the ability to make the right decisions. Being able to self-direct, independently, your own efforts in the direction you choose is very rewarding. If you don't meet your goal in a timely fashion, the only person that you have to answer to is yourself. Additionally, you are able to set your own standards and increase those standards accordingly based on the situations. Being responsible for others, such as your dependents, gives you a lot to strive for and keeps you focused. Since someone is depending on you, your drive to succeed in your endeavors and in managing your responsibilities is enhanced, bringing with it a newfound maturity level and determination. The family is a very important aspect of our community and intact families assist with strengthening them even more. When a person is in a position to work and provide for their family, it brings essential stabilization into the communities.

You serve has a role model

The best way that someone can serve as a role model is just by being a good example, having strength in character, mentoring others and having the right attitude. What is the right attitude? A positive attitude, an attitude that when people look at you, they say, "Wow, I want to be like that person." Having a role model can be the best thing for adolescents and young adults. Unfortunately, not all role models are deserving of the title. Some can steer people in the wrong direction. It's important that a role model understands that he or she can make a difference in the lives of many simply by their actions and their reputation as a successful person. While growing up, I had different role models who made an impression on me based on their personality, their scholastic achievements, athletic abilities, or even their ability to gain the attention of the females. I also had some great role models in my family. For example, my grandfather gave me a great sense of what family togetherness really stood for. He was the leader of our immediate family and extended family as well. He could be counted on to provide support for the family in various ways. He was stern, hardworking and always available when someone in the family needed assistance either financially or for moral support. This instilled in me the firm understanding of the importance of his role in our family. My brother, who was very close in age to me, was also a great role model for me as he was very studious in school, made the dean's list regularly and even worked while in HS, keeping his grades up despite having to balance his academic and work schedule. Having the ability to earn money during the school year also gave him the ability to purchase school clothes and things he wanted for enter-tainment without having to ask my mother for an allowance. That experience was something I wish I had. However, I wasn't as studious in HS as I later became in college when I realized how important it was to graduate on time, achieve academic success and begin to earn a living so I could take care of my family. When I graduated from Marist College at the age of 21, I was already married with two infant sons and ready to excel in the business world.

Earn a living doing what you love

In order to succeed and move in the direction of doing what you love, you have to first really under-stand and identify what you love. When someone is passionate about what they love and how they're able to help people or solve problems, then doing what they love is just going to come naturally. If you focus on money, you may not obtain the money that you want, but if you focus on what it is that you love doing, the money will come. When I graduated from college and entered the workforce, I had aspirations of being an Account Executive on Wall Street, working for one of the major financial institutions in the country. Having prior sales experience was one of the prerequisites I was told I needed in order to get a position as an Account Executive. So since the role I truly wanted wasn't obtainable at the time, that's the direction I took. As I began my career in sales and worked for many companies in a variety of industries, I found myself always fascinated with how the capital markets worked and how wealth was obtained in this country and throughout the world. My experience as a sales professional prepared me to really go for what I wanted in life, kept me driven to reach and exceed my goals and provided me with a career which afforded me the opportunity to raise my family.

I believe we are all in the sales profession in that we must sell our ideas, encourage others to agree with our line of thinking and persuade people to follow us as leaders. I'm grateful to be in the position to do what I love doing in my career today. As an entrepreneur I am fulfilling a dream I always had of being in business for myself and making an impact on the lives of many. Unfortunately, not everyone can say the same. You can probably think of a lot of people you know who are unhappy with the jobs they have, are worried about job security and perhaps are underpaid for the value they bring to a company. These are the times we are living in now in which a majority of people are living paycheck to paycheck. They don't feel they could retire from their current job, or they don't have the job of their choice and are seeking a better way of life. Developing a plan of action to make a transition from your current job to one which provides more satisfaction is a goal many individuals wish they had. If you really desire to make a change or transition from employee to entrepreneur, it's up to you to focus and implement that plan of action. It is possible!! You have to really believe in yourself and go out and make it happen!

Your mind will always be utilized

You have to be involved in stimulating activities. Understand that everything comes from the mind. Focus on positive energy and surround yourself with positive people and positive activities. The stimulation from your environment and from your interactions with people will keep your mind stimulated. Having the ability to create ideas to grow in your profession or reach additional goals in life stems directly from what you're thinking about and what you wish to achieve. Having ambitious thoughts drives people and can propel you to obtain any achievement you set out to achieve. I see far too many individuals who remain in their comfort zone and settle for mediocrity instead of stretching their vison, allowing themselves to continue growing through personal development and maximizing their full potential. Unfortunately, people tend to give up when the going gets tough opposed to sticking it out and using our innate mental toughness to figure out how to achieve the level of satisfaction we desire. When I was faced with a decision to either complete my college education or go get a job to begin taking care of my family, I could have easily decided to do one or the other. Instead, I decided to do both by utilizing my mind to figure out how I could go to classes from 8:30 AM to 2:30 PM then go to work from 4:00PM to 12 Midnight. Was it easy? Absolutely not! However, I was determined to succeed and I didn't want to put myself in a position where I wasn't handling my full responsibilities as a father and student simultaneously. That experience showed me and gave me additional confidence in myself that I could handle pressure and stand up to the adversity I was faced with. Additionally, it showed my family that I wouldn't allow anything to stand in the way of me taking care of them and fulfilling the goals I set out to achieve.

You have the opportunity to change lives

Opportunities change lives. Whether it is a business opportunity, an opportunity to be mentored by someone or to participate in a positive activity, people are able to grow, to help others and to take their business to another level when opportunities are presented. Maybe they even get a vision and through that vision, they are able to realize their dreams. Having an impact on someone's life is huge. As we look at the pressures in society, it is difficult to get ahead and properly take advantage of our free-enterprise system. But with the proper direction from others, it is possible to get ahead. I can see how people who don't have inner drive and ambition can falter in a society like ours. Given the circumstances which exist, mentors who are able to share their knowledge, time and talents with others can make a huge impact in their cooperative initiatives.

Earlier in my career, I was given the opportunity to work for a legend in entrepreneurship and the business world, Mr. Earl G. Graves of Black Enterprise Magazine. As a result of that experience and seeing how the publication featured many other entrepreneurs and successful business entities across this country and the world, I visualized myself being a business owner and succeeding as an entrepreneur one day and being in a position to leave a legacy for my family.

Build your own security

It's so important to build your own security in our society. As we've been accustomed to the notion of going to school, getting a good education and then preparing for a life of working for someone else as a means of security, we are now finding out that this path isn't really secure in most instances. Certainly it's viable to get an education and even gather some relevant work experience in the corporate world, non-profit world or even internship experience. At the same time, depending on one source of income or fulfilling others' dreams by working the duration of your career for someone else isn't in my opinion a secure method. Opposed to being dependent on being an employee and searching for jobs, I feel developing jobs and creating multiple streams of income are certainly more efficient ways of developing sustainable income and establishing security for yourself and your family. There will be risks for working for yourself and developing a business which provides you with the security you wish to obtain. However, after the groundwork has been laid and the business generates exponential growth, the ability to have security can be realized. Where people come up short is when the business has to overcome adversity, challenges and growing pains and you may not see the light at the end of the tunnel. This is a time when you must dig down deep and persevere to understand that the struggle is a part of the process and inevitably you will reach a level of business success which can't be taken from you because your business has developed a structure, scale and expansion which creates stability and security. When you think about an unlimited income potential and becoming wealthy by obtaining financial independence, you have a much better opportunity to reach that level by developing and creating your own security. The satisfaction of accomplishing this feat is monumental. Look at the millionaires of our society. A majority of them have built their empires through multiple streams of income, dedication to their life's purpose and an unwavering commitment to make a difference. They have a vision and leverage their expertise which they can really be proud of. Dr. Claud Anderson is an advocate for taking control of your destiny and ensuring you can provide for yourself and your family through entrepreneurial endeavors, cooperative economics and self-determination to secure your present circumstances as well as your future security in life.

CHAPTER TWO

Wake Up with Purpose Daily and Be Relentless

"I had to make my own living and my own opportunity.
Don't sit down and wait for the opportunities to come.
Get up and make them"
—Madam CJ Walker

Prioritize your daily tasks and set a schedule

Daily tasks are important in that it keeps you focused on what it is that you need to do and identifies the things that are necessary. Outlining your daily tasks helps you with your time management as opposed to aimlessly just floundering around the day and thinking or being reactive versus proactive. Identifying your tasks is going to help you proactively reach certain goals, and as those goals are reached and met, it builds confidence to continue going about your day. If you don't have those daily tasks in place, it can lead to frustration as you move in different directions and perhaps not the direction you want to move in on that given day. Distractions can derail your day and take you in directions you don't want to go in, stagnating your daily growth. When distractions play a part in your day's activities, it makes you feel as though you've been busy. However, what you must take into consideration is your level of progress in the given day. For example, let's say you've dedicated yourself to making a number of calls during the first two hours of your day to schedule appointments. Instead, you check your email, handle personal calls for family situations or catch up on paperwork. You've certainly been busy opposed to being productive and fulfilling your goal. After the two hours are up, you realize you've only scheduled three appointments. The phone gets heavy, meaning you want to make the calls, but it becomes easier to do something else opposed to staying focused on your mission. Self-discipline and holding yourself accountable will allow you to stay the course. Be relentless with your pursuit and maximize your time in an efficient manner. As I've coached individuals in my organization to stay committed to reaching certain activity levels for daily progress, I've had to show them by example what it means to be relentless in my pursuit for accomplishing daily goals. The mantra of 'practice what you preach' holds very true in the business world and if you as a leader don't keep that sustainable behavior, your team will see that you're not as committed as you want them to be.

Inspire your children to be their own boss and work for themselves

The best way to start is by giving them ideas on just small business opportunities. You know, the standard lemonade stand or selling Girl Scout cookies. It all begins with identifying that you can earn a living versus taking a salary or trading time for money. By watching you solve problems and take initiatives, they will develop that mindset early on. As a result, they will focus on being more self-sufficient as opposed to dependent on a job or on someone telling them how much money they can make. It's never too early to begin the process of enlightening your children to the world of entrepreneurship and the business world. I'm a firm believer that business and communications make the world go around. In the society we live in, there are some people who work for themselves, creating jobs and opportunities. On the other hand, there are others who work for big business and are guided by the direction of their employer, dictating the tasks to do as well as the amount of money they will be paid for doing it.

There are many programs and organizations available which teach our youth how to start, own and operate their own businesses. One which comes to mind and has been around for many years is NFTE (National Foundation for Teaching Entrepreneurship), founded by Steve Mariotti. This international, non-profit organization, provides entrepreneurship training and education programs. During its long history, it has exposed many youth to the basics of business formation, encouraging them that they can be in control of their destiny through entrepreneurial endeavors. Early in my career I had the opportunity to be a NFTE instructor and as a result, was able to share the program with my children. Passing down information to my children about business and finance is something which was second nature for me. My mother was a banker for her entire career. As she raised my brother and me, she instilled a keen understanding of business, managing money, the principles of economics and the importance of prioritizing your necessities versus your wants. Naturally, when I became a parent, I passed down the same information to my children. Now that they are parents with children of their own, they have the benefit of understanding the same principles which were passed down to me. There's an enormous amount of benefit our children receive when they are exposed to entrepreneurship and economic education. As they develop into young adults and begin to start their respective careers, they have a foundation of creating activities, developing sources of income, understanding budgeting and fiscal responsibility. Unfortunately, this information isn't mandatory to be taught in all states across our country. Therefore, some youth won't be exposed to this type of learning until they are faced with making these decisions for themselves and in a lot of cases, they are unprepared.

As fathers lead their families, along with the assistance of their spouse or significant other, providing the children this information will prepare them with the necessary life skills to raise a family of their own one day.

Teach your children the importance of communication, marketing and sales

The best way is to encourage your children to express themselves—express themselves when they agree with someone or express themselves when maybe they don't agree. Show them that by expressing themselves, it's important that they get their point across, and it's also going to help them develop listening skills. Marketing is a big part of business; a big part of how you promote or advertise. It's a big part of how you get your messages across. By teaching your children these skill sets, it will generate in their mind that they can promote themselves, they can promote an idea or they can promote sales. All businesses are generated through sales. Without sales, you will not have business expansion. Understanding selling techniques and that we're all in sales will help your children understand that that skill set will take them very far in life. It will also give them the opportunity to obtain the things that they want in life. When you consider companies which grow to multi-million and multi-billion dollar companies, usually the CEO or President of the company rose to the top through the ranks of the sales channel. Sales is the core of the profitability of the company, therefore the sales function has an integral part of the growth, development and expansion of a company. As you teach children the importance of sales, children get to acquire an essential skill which can make them very marketable in their career or their role as an entrepreneur.

Show your children the value of team work

The best way to show your children the value of teamwork is to explain that you can't do it all by yourself. If you have others helping you, you get a lot more done during a period of time because we only have 24 hours in a day. If you have ten people working on a project for four hours, that will generate 40 hours' worth of work. If you are by yourself, doing the same job, you will have limited output. Each person on a team has their own strengths and by combining those different strengths, the work can be expedited or realized a lot quicker. With teamwork, people are able to learn from one another and as ideas come about through the team's efforts, the efforts of the team will be fulfilled. The key message here is that by bringing like-minded individuals together, working in unison for a business, cause or project, the likelihood of success increases tremendously. Developing a Mastermind Group is a viable way to bring like-minded individuals together for a purpose or mission and an excellent way to monitor your process by keeping each other accountable to your common goal. It's never too early to expose your children to high level thinking which generates thought provoking opportunities.

Build a reputation

A person builds a reputation by their activities and actions, by the success that they have in business or in communicating their thoughts for example, or maybe in giving back to society. All of these factors create a positive reputation. As the saying goes, "You have one time to make a good first impression." The reputation you build for yourself can open doors for you. Conversely, a negative reputation will close doors and cause you to miss out on opportunities. Throughout life, people are constantly being rated, judged and treated a certain way based on reputation. Since this is the case, having the wherewithal to maintain a positive reputation is certainly in your best interest. Keep in mind though that you can maintain a good reputation and a careless mistake can cause it to be tarnished. It's important to be cognizant of your behaviors, actions and activities throughout the various experiences in life.

CHAPTER THREE

Work Smarter, Not Harder

"Intellectual growth should commence at birth
and cease only at death."
—*Albert Einstein*

Plan your day the night before

It's important to plan your day the night before because it gives you an understanding of what business that you have to do when you wake up; you're ready. You are not spending time thinking about what it is that you have to do. If you develop a plan once the day has already begun, you may get distracted and in fact be less productive. Overcoming distractions takes time away from your plan. Additionally, when you plan your day the night before, you are more focused on what you want to accomplish. As you accomplish these tasks or activities, you can check them off, building your confidence knowing that you achieved what you set out to achieve. Maximizing your time on a daily basis sets an example that being efficient increases your level of production.

Track your time

Time management is very important if you want to be efficient in what it is that you want to accomplish. By tracking your time, you are directing your energy level and prioritizing what is most important to get that done first. If you're not tracking your time, you might be aimlessly going about your day. When you look back at your accomplishments, you want to be able to gauge how much time did it take to accomplish a specific activity. As you plan the rest of your week, you want to know how much time you need to allocate for those activities that are going to generate maximum results. The saying that 'time is money' is very true. If you utilize your time properly, you can effectively make more money and have more time for your family.

Tracking your time is going to increase your efficiency. Aside from helping you to allocate your time effectively, it also gives you confidence that you're able to build upon each task and to finish it completely. You want to expedite your time as much as possible, and if you don't track it, then you can be distracted by other things that come into play. When you have distractions, it lowers your effectiveness for the day.

Avoid procrastination by creating micro-goals

Procrastination is something that a lot of people are faced with. If you have a big goal to accomplish, you can break that goal down into mini-goals. By breaking a large goal down into smaller pieces, it encourages you to tackle and achieve each goal. At first glance, a large goal may seem daunting and may in fact prevent you from starting and putting those activities in place necessary to achieve it. By alleviating the procrastination through establishing and fulfilling micro-goals, you will build your confidence to continue on to the next.

Focus on consistent progress

You definitely need to focus on consistent progress. Moving forward is certainly important. Thinking about past mistakes can prevent you from thinking and moving forward. Thinking about the future and creating that future generates confidence and the ability to have further fulfillment in your life. It generates the ability to share with others and to show how you can make a difference in forward-moving progress, career advancement or business expansion. As you move forward, roadblocks may come in your path. However, it's important to not let any obstacles derail your progress. Staying focused on your ultimate goal despite the obstacles is critical. We can get sidetracked at times or lose momentum at a point when you are very close to achieving a goal. Determination wins! Keep your eye on the prize until you obtain what you aspire to achieve.

Leverage your networking relationships

In order to leverage your networking relationships, build your network. Consciously work on providing resources to your network and not just looking for your network to provide resources to you. Building and generating mutually beneficial interactions and relationships is key to leveraging your network You want to be able to reciprocate assistance or services to someone in need, giving you access to resources in various ways as well.

Learn from others

You want to learn from others because you grow by learning. If you just live in your own vacuum, then you're only as good as whatever skill set that you have. By learning from others and different experiences, you build upon your own skills. There's always something that you're going to learn. Whether it's a negative or positive experience, it's going to be a learning experience. You can take others' strengths and build them upon your own. You can also take others' weaknesses and learn that that's not something that you want to adhere to. Focus on someone's strengths as opposed to developing weaknesses within yourself. Learning from others helps you then be able to teach others as the tire turns. You learn it and you're able to teach.

CHAPTER FOUR

Constantly Take Action

"Firms need to ensure that their ability to provide effective customer service keeps pace with their growth. If you're marketing your firm to new customers, you better be able to provide them service when they do business with you."
—*Arthur Levitt, Former Chairman of the US Securities and Exchange Commission*

Inform a keen sense of observation and self-drive

Being self-driven is important. Sometimes you can get frustrated. Sometimes things don't go your way or obstacles get in the way of you reaching your goals. However, the first thing you have to do is really be keen as to what it is that you want, what you're looking to establish or what it is that you're looking to achieve. Being reactive versus proactive slows down your progress. If you're not driven and really don't have that self-motivation, sometimes it can get you down when disappointments set in. You've got to keep on going regardless of what obstacles may be in your way.

Visualize goals

First of all, goal-setting is very important. If you don't know where you're going, and you don't know what you want to achieve, then you may not move in the right direction. If you visualize first and you can see what it is you want to obtain, you will get closer to obtaining it versus just aimlessly going about your day. I've found that when I write down my plan and my goals and create action plans to achieve them, I'm more likely to achieve those goals. If I don't plan it, then I'm not focusing on my goals. Sometimes you have to readjust your goals. If you don't have goals in the first place, then you're not moving forward. Goals are a driving force for many people, especially those who are ambitious, competitive and aggressive in nature. As you work on achieving your goals and you reach a level of success in accomplishing some goals, it gives you encouragement, satisfaction and confidence to continue setting goals and knowing you have the ability to reach them. I have found that when I aspire for something important to me, I do whatever it takes to obtain it. At times though, I have to exert patience because the goal isn't always reached on the first attempt. This is where mental toughness plays a part in your life. Reaching your goals isn't always easy and obstacles can at times stand in the way. The strong survive throughout whatever obstacles they may be faced with and are provided with a learning experience.

Exercise – maintain good health

Exercising and maintaining good health is very critical to your success. Without your health, it's very difficult to move about in your life. Having good health and maintaining an exercise regimen is going to increase your level of energy, fight off disease and help you stay and look in good shape. People will want to be around you or be in your presence because they can see that you are a healthy individual. When your appearance is positive, sharp, it helps people who may see the potential in you, to help them see the potential in themselves. But overall, a healthy person usually gets more done. As an individual is focused on increasing levels of activity to get more done and be prosperous, the healthy lifestyle you must have is determined by many factors: Proper nutrition, consistent work outs and managing your stress level. Being in business for yourself can be very stressful at times, especially when you are in the building stages of the business. Working long hours, delegating duties and managing the daily activities of business development can be very strenuous. It's very important to stay in good physical shape to weather the demands of being an entrepreneur or business owner.

Who's your customer – targeting is key

In business, you must know who it is that you're looking to solve that problem for. As you deliver a message, you want to know who it is that you are delivering that message to. Targeting allows you to focus on who can benefit from your product or service and to generate the message appropriately.

It also gives you the ability to develop better skills. Do not try to please a large group versus targeting and narrowing down who will most benefit from what it is that you have to offer. It's critical to really understand what problems they may have that you can solve. As you develop your target market, providing value for what they are looking for makes your job much easier. Individuals prefer to purchase what it is they are looking for opposed to being sold on a product or service. As you identify who is searching for your product or service, business is then consummated.

Provide value – don't sell

The best way to provide value and not sell is really honing in on your listening skills, really being able to understand someone's weakness, pain points or dissatisfaction. Then you will be able to come up with solutions or a remedy. Sometimes people don't want to be sold to, but rather they want to buy what it is that they're looking for. You've got to identify what someone's looking for or what they're lacking, and then provide the value of fulfilling what it is that they're looking for. I recall early in my career, a hiring manager asked me during an interview, "What is the most important attribute a successful salesperson should possess"? I responded with being a persuasive talker. The hiring manager responded that although that is certainly a good attribute to have, a much better attribute and a skill which will take you much further in your career in sales is attentively listening to the decision maker and understanding what he/she is looking to achieve or receive which your product or service offers. There lies the key. How can you bring value to the decision maker? When this is accomplished, the sale occurs. Business transactions are established and long term relationships are developed through understanding the unique value proposition.

Manage risk

It's important to take risks in business. Those who have achieved success in business have taken risks. At the same time, it's important to manage those risks, especially if you have to invest in startup costs. You want to get a return on your investment.

If you don't properly understand what the risks are, and you don't manage those risks appropriately, you could lose. By managing those risks and understanding them, you are more likely to win. Once you understand what the risks are, you can effectively put and implement a plan to overcome whatever risk that you may be faced with.

CHAPTER FIVE

Build Your a Team

"Growth is never by mere chance; it is the
result of forces working together
—James Cash Penney, Founder of JC Penney

Lead by example

You want to lead by example especially if you are looking to build a team. If you have a goal that you want to achieve, you've got to do it first if you want others to follow and do it along with you. It's important that you set that positive example. Lead first and then teach others to follow. You will get a lot more accomplished. The power of a team is exciting, monumental and generates exponential growth. As your team is developing, new business partners coming onboard and goals of your business are established. The dynamics of building your team will get your adrenaline flowing. As the leader of your team, various skill sets are required to exhibit leadership acumen. Having a no-excuse mentality for yourself and your team members is one aspect of leadership which will propel your team to greatness. Additionally taking the responsibility of ensuring your team members hold themselves accountable for their actions will give each team member a level of assurance that they can succeed no matter what circumstances they may face while conducting business and building relationships. Lastly, instilling in your team the mental toughness which is necessary to compete at the highest level and never give up is what makes building a team so rewarding.

Envision the big picture to inspire passion

Visualizing the big picture is important because you want to begin with the end in mind. If you begin with the end in mind, you then are able to understand what it is going to take to reach the ultimate goal. Once you have a visualization of what it is that you want to accomplish, you might see that that is something that you're passionate about. As you show passion for what you want to accomplish, it gets contagious. You want to encourage others to do the same. When people are passionate about what they want to achieve, their confidence is built, their self-esteem is enhanced, and they know that they're doing something for their own good as well as for others.

By envisioning the big picture with the understanding of your ultimate goal, it will move you in that direction. If you are passionate, people working with you to reach that goal or see that vision will be able to actualize that vision more easily. If you don't show passion, then people may not be motivated to really go after that actual big goal. If they see your passion and they develop it themselves, then together it can be a cohesive effort to fulfill the ultimate goal. It's important to visualize that end result keep it in mind as you go about your daily life to actually reach that ultimate goal.

Collaborate locally

Collaborating helps to spread out the activity. It helps to enhance a project or business development. If you have ten people working on a project versus one or two, you're able to get more done. Everyone has their own strengths and by building upon the strengths and activities of others to fulfill a project or a goal or expand a business, it's going to help expedite that project. If you have to do it all on your own, you could make mistakes, and as you make mistakes you've got to overcome those mistakes. Therefore, it'll take you longer to actually reach what you're looking to accomplish. From the standpoint of seeking out assistance in business, it can be very helpful when you can generate synergistic business partners and establish alliances which generates greater profitability for all parties. This is evident when your partnerships are able to produce additional value added services or additional products which can be brought to market.

Everybody should be rowing in
the same direction

It's important to row in the same direction. If you have people going in different directions, you're going to have disagreements and arguments. It can also lead to dysfunction within the team. Understanding where you're going is the first step.

But understanding that everyone must move in the same direction is the second step. Then you need to monitor that everyone's moving in the same direction. If people are not, you must be able to identify them and then give them a choice of whether they want to continue participating or not. From a business standpoint, having a mission or goals to obtain with your business, you want to have business partners who believe in the same thing you believe in and are delivering the same message when marketing your product or service. If you have different partners delivering various messages of the features and benefits of the product or service, you run the risk of confusion in the marketplace. Developing a consistent message which combats the features and benefits of your competitors will propel your business growth. As your message resonates with your client base and prospective clients, the referrals you obtain as a result will be indicative of a solid value proposition, consistent message and superior customer service. This will only occur when all business associates are on the same page, moving in the same direction.

Focus on your people more than you focus on your customers

By focusing on your people and not just your customers, and in developing your people, ultimately you are going to be able to help your customers. If you build your people up and enhance their skills, you're better able to meet your customers' needs. If you just focus on the customers, your people may not be able to deliver what it is that your customers want. Enhancing and developing leaders within your team helps to expedite the growth of your business or your team's success. Their character needs to be built, their integrity needs to be enhanced, their listening skills need to be developed, and their salesmanship needs to be realized as they move forward with helping the customer. As you develop leaders within your organization, the leadership qualities which you have passed down to your leadership team will ultimately trickle down to the next layer of leaders. The continuum of leadership development is relevant and the team leadership dynamics play a major role in the overall growth and expansion of the business. If the transference of leadership skills doesn't continue to be passed down to the next level, you may lose some of your essential important team members in the process. In the world of business, the team focus is essential for sustainability, relationship building and rapport within the ranks.

Bolster effective communication skills

Communication makes the world go 'round. Most of your communication skills are going to allow you to interact with different people and about different subject matter, which will allow you to effectively be able to interact with more people. By interacting with more people, you will be able to count on those people, to bring those people on your team or to effectively get your message across. As we live our lives, communicating is so important since everything relies on communication. It can be written, verbal, or physical in terms of body language. There are different forms of communication, but they all need to be enhanced in order to effectively get what you want to accomplish.

CHAPTER SIX

Understand How to Course Correct

"The greatest danger in times of turbulence is not the turbulence – it is to act with yesterday's logic"
—*Peter Drucker*

Record your expectations

You want to record their expectations because you're able to manage your expectations. In order to manage your expectations, you have to know what those expectations are. As you record your expectations, you can then implement a plan of action. You know what it takes to get to what it is that you expect, but it's critical to put that road map in place. Then you're able to monitor that road map as you go along. Initial goals may be established for a business to succeed. During the course of executing your business plan, certain outcomes will go as planned. At the same time, you have to be prepared to change course or make adjustments to the plan because of a change in market conditions or a new entrant into the market as competition. A disruption within your company's product or service can derail your business productivity for a short period of time or a much longer period of time depending on the severity of the situation.

Don't ignore the problems

Ignoring a problem only creates a bigger problem. We can't get around that problems exist, and business development is generated by solving problems. If you don't identify the problem first, it's just going to manifest into other things. Therefore you want to work on alleviating that problem because you can't ignore it. If a problem goes unaddressed and gets out of hand, it's going to require more work and more effort to get things back on track. Ignoring problems takes a lot of time away from you fulfilling what it is that you want to fulfill.

Address problems with facts

By addressing problems with the facts, then you're crystal clear on solving the problem. Base your decisions for the changes that you're making on facts rather than opinions. This way you're able to justify how things need to be changed based on proof. Although this may have been the initial direction, based on the facts, you may need to make a change. If you're basing it just on opinions, that's all it is, someone's opinion. Everyone's entitled to their own opinion, but someone's opinion can be wrong versus the facts which can be substantiated by proof.

You must be willing to adjust

You should be willing to adjust. Not everything is going to go right all the time. You want to move in the right direction, of course, but sometimes it's a necessity to make changes to make improvements. If you're going down a wrong path, and you keep going down that wrong path, the end result is going to be wrong. However, if you make adjustments and

47

are flexible, you can change the direction and get to your goal or be able to solve your problem. If you don't adjust, then it creates a larger problem.

Set consequences if things don't change

It's important to set consequences. Without consequences, then there's no stimulus to change in certain instances. If you don't put standards in place and people don't adhere to those standards, then they're going to keep doing whatever they want to do. If it's necessary to make changes to course correct, there has to be a consequence to make sure that people know that they will lose out on something. Consequences help people realize that they need to make a change.

CHAPTER SEVEN

Support Giving Back to Society

"Surround yourself with only people who are
going to lift you higher"
—*Oprah Winfrey*

Share your skills and experiences

By sharing your skills and experiences, you're able to teach, and people are able to learn from you. You're able to pave the way for someone else to follow after you. By sharing your experiences, you are in essence building your reputation. It helps to show the value that you're able to offer someone for them to benefit from, learn from, or to make an impact on the lives of others. As you look to grow and prosper, one of the best ways to do so is to give of yourself to enable others to learn from your expertise. In doing so, you will continue to grow and along the way you are able to show a path of success for someone else. In our society, you have a lot of people who are out for themselves and aren't earnestly thinking of the next person because it's hard enough to make it on your own. What I've found is that once you give of yourself and share what you have regardless of how much it is, you and others benefit tremendously from your acts of generosity and sharing.

Pave the way for others

It's important to pave the way for others because people are looking at you and people have paved the way for you. When you look at history, people have died to make things better and give others the opportunity to achieve academic and business success, or just the basic thing of voting. As people have paved the way for you, it's important to give back and to pave the way for others, maybe as a cameo effect. Then others will continue paving the way for others, as well.

Develop your legacy

I believe developing a legacy is very important. It's something that is developed through either business endeavors or within your family. It is something that helps to change lives and to expand your reputation. It helps to future generations something to be proud of, something to know that as a result of your efforts, you've made life better for them. From a family standpoint or from a business standpoint, it's something that will never end. It will be perpetual, giving you the ability to affect generation after generation. When I think of a person who has provided her family with a legacy to be proud of, I think of Madam CJ Walker, one of the first women self-made millionaires through her entrepreneurial endeavors, business creativity and invention of hair care products. Another individual who comes to mind is Nelson Mandela, who was imprisoned for 27 years. After serving those years, he eventually became the President of South Africa and his legacy is etched in history as a phenomenal leader who persevered through struggle, adversity and institutional racism. My legacy is continuing to evolve. As a former corporate business development professional and now currently an entrepreneur, I'm establishing my legacy through my accomplishments, family expansion and my community service activities. Each of us has an opportunity to leave a legacy which our families can be proud of. What will your legacy be?

Generational Succession Planning

Generational succession planning is designed to pass down skill sets and businesses to the next generation. Generational wealth can be passed down, giving people the ability to grow their respective families. They're able to make a larger impact on society. They're able to give the next generation a good start rather than them having to start from scratch. It gives them a blueprint for succeeding and carrying on what was already established and preserving a legacy which can never be taken away.

Generational succession planning helps to pave the way for the next generation coming behind you. You want to make it transformational, impacting the next generation. You want to be able to pass down generational wealth and leaders within your family or within your business who can continue the work that has been done. You may want to continue certain traditions and continue to make an impact on society based on the efforts that your forefathers have put in place. It gives the next generation a better start in life and the ability to make decisions as to whether they want to continue in the same path or make changes. It's better to have that choice than to not have any choice at all.

Conclusion

The reason for writing this book was to provide a blueprint for individuals who desire to understand the importance of entrepreneurship in our society. In particular, how developing a mindset to learn business fundamentals, sales and marketing concepts and how fathers can play an instrumental role in assisting their children with a better understanding of entrepreneurial endeavors. We live in a society in which the focus has been on getting a great education and working to develop a career to earn a living and to raise a family. This option has its benefits. However, at the same time, it can have drawbacks if it's the individual's sole path to earning an income. As competition for jobs in our society continues to increase, and because we live in a very capitalistic society, maintaining and raising a family today can be very stressful. There is also added pressure to choose the right partner who is compatible with us as individuals, while also having harmonious thoughts and actions about raising a family, earning an income and leading the family. This requires major commitments from both heads of households.

With so much pressure to succeed, lead families and fulfill the many responsibilities of life, keeping families together creates challenges for all of us. Unfortunately, this ability to keep families together in our society has been problematic. Certainly, there are various factors which contribute to the deterioration of the family structure. For example, a major contributor is a lack of sustainable income. Having a sustainable income which is created through self-initiatives, entrepreneurial endeavors and multiple streams of income, can develop a sense of security in the home versus having only one source of income through a job alone.

Small business ownership is a driving force behind a thriving economy providing people with the ability to contribute to the growth and development of their community; it also provides them with the means to take care of their families, educate their children, purchase homes, and maintain a lifestyle of their choice. As the divorce rate continues to increase and the number of single-parent households rises, additional pressures are placed on individuals to lead their families. We must find solutions to this ever-increasing problem. My experience witnessing my mother single-handedly raise my brother and me gave me a first-hand view of the pressure of single-headed households. This encouraged my commitment to teach my children the principles of entrepreneurship, developing an income through self-initiatives and staying committed to taking care of their children as they raise their families.

The leadership skills required to raise a family, balance a career or business and keep your family together have many benefits for our communities. Strengthening our communities through stable families, two-parent households, and individuals with secure incomes creates harmonious relationships and certainly can reduce crime in our society. As children see their parents live harmoniously and in loving relationships, it builds self-esteem and character-building principles for the entire family, creating additional stability in our communities.

When children lack self-esteem, are exposed to negative images and disunity in their family, they tend to be faced with challenges which can be devastating and traumatic. Having a sense of direction from both parents and especially seeing strength from their father can have tremendous positive effects for children and their future. When a family can overcome adversity through effective communication, conflict resolution and problem-solving skills under the leadership of both parents, an optimal family structure exists. As fathers are able to maintain their place in the household, providing their children with the necessary skills to succeed in all facets of their lives, I believe there will be a decrease in the divorce rate, an increase in the rate of stable families and perhaps a greater percentage of thriving communities. Having a better understanding of economic principles, understanding how businesses are formed and operated certainly can provide our children a foundation for succeeding in our society.

Each of us has been provided with God given talents. With an increase in our self-esteem, proper direction and a focused vision, the ability to live a purpose driven life can be fulfilled. To have faith in oneself that you can develop a business for yourself which enables sustainability for your family is a very rewarding experience. Having a business which can be passed down from generation to generation creates an everlasting legacy for a family and gives each generation a succession plan of economic stability, making a powerful impact on society.